Help the Environment

Cleaning up Litter

Charlotte Guillain

Heinemann Library
Chicago Illinois

Customer Service 888-454-2279

Visit our website at www.heinemannraintree.com

Picture research: Erica Martin, Hannah Taylor and Ginny Stroud-Lewis
Designed by Philippa Jenkins
Printed and bound in China by South China Printing Company.
12 11 10 09
10 9 8 7 6 5 4 3 2

Library of Congress Cataloging-in-Publication Data
Guillain, Charlotte.
  Cleaning up litter / Charlotte Guillain.
    p. cm. -- (Help the environment)
  Includes bibliographical references and index.
  ISBN-13: 978-1-4329-0885-0 (hc)
  ISBN-13: 978-1-4329-0891-1 (pb)
  1. Litter (Trash)--Juvenile literature. I. Title.
  TD813.G85 2008
  363.72'8--dc22

                        2007041171

Acknowledgments
The author and publisher would like to thank the following for permission to reproduce photographs: ©Alamy pp. **5** (Gari Wyn Williams), **6**, **23 middle** (ilian), **8** (Jeff Greenberg), **4 bottom left** (Kevin Foy), **17** (Mark Boulton), **11** (Peter Glass), **4 top right**, **23 top** (Westend 61); ©ardea.com pp. **12** (Don Hadden), **14** (Valeria Taylor); ©Brand X Pixtures p. **4 bottom right** (Morey Milbradt); ©Corbis p. **22** (Philip James Corwin); ©Digital Vision p. **4 top left**; ©Getty Images p. **18** (Blend Images); ©PA Photos p. **15** (DPA Deutsche Press-Agentur, DPA); ©Photodisc p. **7**; ©Photoeditinc. pp. **9** (Cindy Charles), **20** (Tony Freeman); ©Photolibrary pp. **19**, **23 bottom** (Bill Bachman Photography), **10** (Brandx Pictures), **21** (Deyoung Michael), **13** (Digital Vision), **16** (John Brown).

Cover photograph of a child putting litter in a bin reproduced with permission of ©Superstock (PhotoAlto). Back cover photograph of a girl picking up a bottle reproduced with permission of ©Alamy (Mark Boulton).

Every effort has been made to contact copyright holders of any material reproduced in this book.
Any omissions will be rectified in subsequent printings if notice is given to the publishers.

Contents

What Is the Environment?

The environment is the world
all around us.

We need to care for
the environment.

What Is Litter?

Litter is things that we do
not need any more.

Litter is bad for the environment.

Ways to Help the Environment

When we pick up litter,
we clean up the world.
8 We help the environment.

When we put litter in a trash can,
we clean up the world.
We help the environment.

Sometimes there are no trash cans.

When we take litter with us,
we clean up the world.
We help the environment.

Litter on the ground can
hurt animals.

When we pick up litter,
we help animals.
We help the environment.

Litter in the oceans can hurt animals.

When we pick up litter,
we clean up the ocean.
We help the environment.

Glass on the ground can start
forest fires.

When we pick up glass,
we help stop forest fires.
We help the environment.

Some trash can be recycled.

When we recycle, we make new things from old things.
We help the environment.

We can clean up litter.

We can help the environment.

How Are They Helping?

PLEASE!
HELP KEEP THIS CENTER CLEAN
PLACE RECYCLABLES INSIDE THE DOMES

How are these children helping
the environment?

Answer on p. 24

Picture Glossary

 **environment** the world around us

 **litter** things we do not need any more

 **recycle** make old things into new things

Index

Answer to question on p. 22: The children are helping the environment by recycling cans.

Note to Parents and Teachers

Before reading
Talk to children about what litter is and how it can harm the environment. For example, show them the plastic rings that hold drink cans together. Explain that they can harm animals that get caught in the rings.

After reading
• Make a class poster that says Don't Be a Litter Bug. On one side of the poster, glue some examples of litter that harms the environment. On the other side of the poster, draw pictures of what we can do to make less litter, such as taking litter home with us and recycling.